Mariagrazia Bertarini • Paolo Iotti • Tracey Sinclair

PRONTI PER LA **PROVA**

INVALSI • 5

INGLESE

EDIZIONE 2020

ELI
PUBLISHING

INDICE

Mariagrazia Bertarini, Paolo Iotti, Tracey Sinclair
Pronti per la prova INVALSI 5 – Inglese

Responsabile editoriale: Beatrice Loreti
Responsabile di produzione: Francesco Capitano
Progetto grafico e impaginazione: Andersen
Illustrazioni: Gianluca Martini

Via Brecce, 100 – Loreto
tel. 071 750 701

info@elilaspigaedizioni.it
www.elilaspigaedizioni.it

Stampato in Italia presso
Tecnostampa - Pigini Group Printing Division
Loreto - Trevi
19.83.433.0
ISBN 978-88-468-4006-6

ISTRUZIONI

La prova si compone di <u>due parti</u>. La prima parte è formata da cinque testi che dovrai leggere per poi rispondere alle domande che li seguono. Nella seconda parte dovrai ascoltare cinque brani in inglese e rispondere alle domande che troverai nel fascicolo.
Le istruzioni prima di ogni domanda ti diranno come rispondere. Leggile dunque con molta attenzione. <u>La prima domanda è sempre un esempio.</u> Se ti accorgi di aver sbagliato, puoi correggere: in alcuni casi puoi barrare con una riga la risposta sbagliata e riscrivere quella che ritieni corretta, come negli esempi seguenti:

0	Q1	Q2	Q3	Q4	Q5
F	D	B	A	~~B~~ C	E

0 Where is Mary from?	New York
Q1 What does Mary have for breakfast?	Milk and cereals
Q2 What is Mary's favourite subject?	~~Geography~~ Maths

In caso di scelta tra quattro possibili risposte puoi scrivere **NO** accanto alla risposta che ritieni sbagliata e mettere una crocetta su quella corretta, come negli esempi seguenti:

Q1) Frank is

No A. ☒ Judith's son.
B. ☐ Judith's father.
C. ☒ Judith's brother.
D. ☐ Judith's husband.

A	B	C

YES ☐ NO ☐	YES ☒ NO ☒ No	YES ☒ NO ☐

Per fare una prova, ora rispondi a questa domanda.

Q1) How many months are there in a year?

A. ☐ 4
B. ☐ 10
C. ☒ 12
D. ☐ 14

Per svolgere la prima parte della prova avrai <u>30 minuti</u>. Al termine della prima parte potrai riposarti e riprendere quando ti sarà detto di farlo. La seconda parte della prova durerà <u>circa 30 minuti</u>.

TASK 1

Look at the school map. Read and complete the sentences (1-6).
Write your answers in the right-hand column.
The first one (0) is an example.

Nell'attività dovrai osservare attentamente le scritte e le immagini del disegno e completare alcune frasi nella colonna a destra della tabella. Non avere fretta di rispondere. Ci sono esercizi che a prima vista sembrano complicati, ma diventano più semplici se affrontati con calma e concentrazione.

SCHOOL MAP

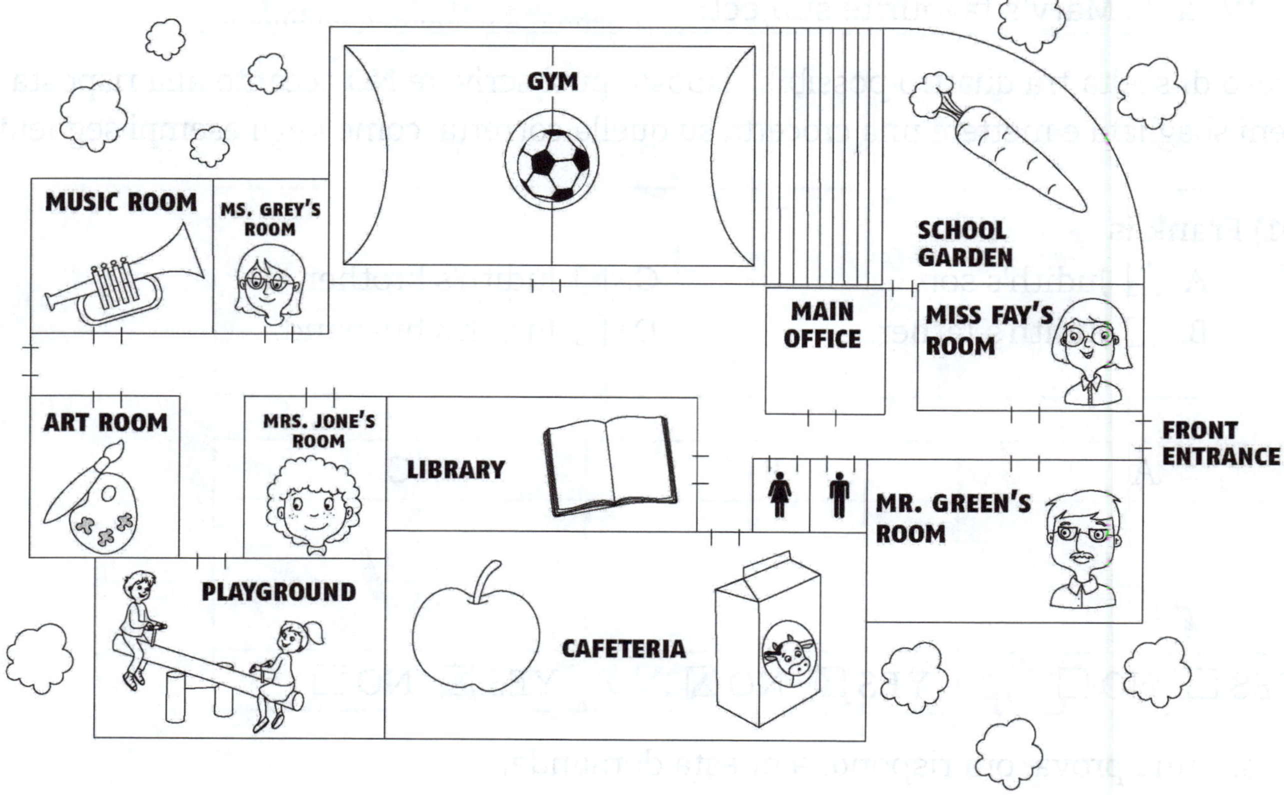

0	*The students are growing vegetables in the _______.*	*school garden*
Q1	Mark is doing sports in the _______.	
Q2	Samuel is having lunch in the _______.	
Q3	Olivia is painting in the _______.	
Q4	The children are playing in the _______.	
Q5	Annabel is practising her violin in the _______.	
Q6	Sophie is reading in the _______.	

Tratto da www.invalsi.it

TASK 2

Read the library signs (A-G) and match them with the sentences (1-5). There is one letter you do not need. Write your answers in the boxes. The first one (0) is an example.

Osserva le immagini, poi leggi le frasi nella tabella. Accanto a ogni frase scrivi la lettera dell'immagine corrispondente. Questa attività richiede concentrazione e spirito di osservazione. Ce la farai certamente!

LIBRARY RULES

A

B

C

D

E

F

G

In a library you

0	*Read and talk quietly.*	C
Q1	Always walk, never run.	
Q2	Don't eat.	
Q3	Can ask the stuff for help.	
Q4	Don't write in the books.	
Q5	Put the books away in their correct places.	

Tratto da www.invalsi.it

TASK 3

Read the text about David who lives in Vevey, Switzerland.
Choose the correct answer (A, B, C, or D) for questions 1-6.
Put a cross (X) in the correct box.
The first one (0) is an example.

Qui dovrai leggere attentamente il testo per rispondere a delle domande. Metti una crocetta vicino alla risposta corretta. Non affrettarti a rispondere, perché in alcuni casi potrebbe esserci un piccolo trabocchetto. Non preoccuparti: se osserverai i dettagli con attenzione, te ne accorgerai sicuramente!

english forum switzerland
In association with The Local

Post Reply

20.11.2011, 17:44

david
Newbie

Join Date: Nov 2011
Location: Vevey
Posts: 5

Hello, My name is David and I live in Vevey. I am new to this forum.

Hello, I am new to this forum and I would like to introduce myself. My name is David Leiser. I am Belgian, 26 years of age and I live in Vevey. I am an engineer. I am interested in yoga, tennis, speaking Spanish and meeting people. If you live in the area and you would like to meet people please get in touch. I am very keen to meet people.

Regards,

David

20.11.2011. 18:05

hannah
Forum Legend

Join Date: Jan 2010
Location: Baden
Posts: 4,594

Re: Hello, My name is David and I live in Vevey. I am new to this forum.

Welcome David!
I don't live near you but hope you soon make lots of new friends! ☺

Quote

PROVA UFFICIALE 2019 FACSIMILE

0 *Where does David live?*

A. ☐ In London.
B. ☐ In Milan.
C. ☐ In Berlin.
D. ☒ *In Vevey.*

Q1) What's his surname?

A. ☐ Newbie.
B. ☐ Leiser.
C. ☐ Legend.
D. ☐ Smith.

Q2) Where is he from?

A. ☐ Germany.
B. ☐ Great Britain.
C. ☐ Spain.
D. ☐ Belgium.

Q3) How old is he?

A. ☐ Twenty-six.
B. ☐ Eleven.
C. ☐ Thirty-two.
D. ☐ Forty-four.

Q4) What's his job?

A. ☐ He is a blogger.
B. ☐ He is a Spanish teacher.
C. ☐ He is an engineer.
D. ☐ He is a university student.

Q5) When does he write this post?

A. ☐ In November.
B. ☐ In January.
C. ☐ In March.
D. ☐ In October.

Q6) Who answer David's post?

A. ☐ Nobody.
B. ☐ His friend John.
C. ☐ Bob Baden.
D. ☐ Hannah.

Tratto da www.invalsi.it

TASK 4

Read the text about visiting different places in London.
Complete the sentences (1-5). Use a maximum of 4 words.
Write your answers in the boxes.
The first one (0) is an example.

Leggi il testo. Cerca le informazioni che ti servono per completare le frasi della tabella. Qui ti viene chiesto di non usare più di quattro parole per ogni completamento. Non avere fretta di rispondere, perché in alcuni casi potrebbe esserci un piccolo inganno. Come sempre, attenzione e concentrazione!

WELCOME TO LONDON AND WELCOME TO THE BIG BUS TOUR

- The Big Bus Sightseeing Tour is a great way to discover London.
- Your ticket lasts for 24 hours and you can board any of the Big Bus open-top buses during this time.
- There are 2 types of tour and you can use both during your day. The Red Tour has a personal guide who provides an entertaining live commentary in English. The Blue Tour provides you with a recorded commentary in a choice of 8 languages. Free headsets are provided.
- Tours run every day except Christmas Day, with regular departures every 15 minutes from 8:30 hrs until 18:00 hrs.

0	*The name of the tour is ______.*	*Big Bus Sightseeing Tour*
Q1	The ticket is ______.	hours
Q2	Number of tour types: ______.	
Q3	The language used on the Red Tour is ______.	
Q4	The first tour of the day is at ______.	hours
Q5	The tours are every ______.	minutes

Tratto da www.invalsi.it

TASK 5

Read the texts about some students (A-G) and match them with the sentences (1-5). There is one letter you do not need.
Write your answers in the boxes.
The first one (0) is an example.

Leggi le descrizioni, osserva le immagini e scrivi accanto a ogni frase la lettera corrispondente. Non preoccuparti se incontri qualche parola nuova; cerca di capire il senso in generale di ogni descrizione e non ti sarà difficile completare l'esercizio correttamente.

WHO LIKES WHAT?

A) 

Craig loves to play football, basketball and baseball with kids in his neighborhood. But his favourite activity is going on the internet during computer classes.

B) 

Allison's favourite subject is math. She likes to do division and multiplication problems for fun.

C) 

For fun, Jaha plays musical instruments. He loves to play African music on his drums. He's played drums for over two years now. He also plays the violin.

D) 

Teiron has fun in his neighborhood, Harlem, where he plays basketball with his friends. Teiron wants to become a teacher and a basketball player when he grows up.

E) 

Micheda loves to swim and play basketball. In the summer, she likes to go on vacations with her family.

Tratto da www.invalsi.it

F) 

Rakeisha loves her neighborhood because there's a playground where she and her brother can play. She likes to play basketball and go holiday parties at the Milbank Center.

G) 

Gaishamar likes to play tag and hide-and-seek with her friends. She also likes to read.

This kid

0	*likes to play football, basketball and baseball.*	A
Q1	loves to go to parties when school is out.	
Q2	likes to go on holiday with mum and dad.	
Q3	loves to play children games.	
Q4	is very good at music.	
Q5	loves to play with numbers.	

TASK 6

FAST FOOD RESTAURANT

Listen to a girl ordering something to eat at a fast food restaurant. While listening, choose the correct answer (A,B,C or D) for questions 1-4. Put a cross (X) in the correct box. Only one answer is correct. The first one (0) is an example. You will hear the recording twice. You will have 20 seconds at the end of the second recording to complete your answers. You now have 20 seconds to look at the task.

Prima di ascoltare la registrazione, leggi le domande e guarda con attenzione le immagini e le scritte; puoi già immaginare molte delle parole che stai per ascoltare. Appena parte la registrazione, fai una crocetta sotto all'immagine che risponde correttamente alla domanda. Ascolterai il testo due volte, perciò non avere fretta. Vedrai che è facile.

0 What's the name of the fast food restaurant?

Pizza Time	Burger Chef	Big Bite	Burger Speed
A ☐	B ☒	C ☐	D ☐

Q1) What does the girl order?

A ☐	B ☐	C ☐	D ☐

Q2) What does she want to drink?

A ☐	B ☐	C ☐	D ☐

Q3) What does she have for dessert?

A ☐	B ☐	C ☐	D ☐

Q4) How much does she pay?

£10	£12	£20	£22
A ☐	B ☐	C ☐	D ☐

Tratto da www.invalsi.it

2

TASK 7

MY HOUSE

Listen to Rachel describing her house. While listening, choose the correct answer (A, B, C or D) for questions 1-5. Put a cross (X) in the correct box. Only one answer is correct. The first one (0) is an example. You will hear the recording twice.
You will have 20 seconds at the end of the second recording to complete your answers.
You now have 20 seconds to look at the task.

Prima dell'ascolto, leggi rapidamente tutte le frasi e i possibili completamenti. Ascolta che cosa ti dice Rachel della sua casa. Mentre ascolti, scegli il completamento giusto ad ogni frase. Anche in questo caso ascolterai il testo due volte, perciò non preoccuparti. Al termine del secondo ascolto avrai ancora un po' di tempo per rispondere al meglio. Ce la farai!

0 *Rachel lives in*
- A. ☐ a castle.
- B. ☐ a flat.
- C. ☒ *a house.*
- D. ☐ a cottage.

Q1) The house is
- A. ☐ big.
- B. ☐ small.
- C. ☐ old.
- D. ☐ new.

Q2) Rachel's favourite room is
- A. ☐ the kitchen.
- B. ☐ the bedroom.
- C. ☐ the bathroom.
- D. ☐ the study.

Q3) In her room Rachel uses
- A. ☐ the computer.
- B. ☐ the mobile phone.
- C. ☐ the tablet.
- D. ☐ the camera.

Q4) The dog likes
- A. ☐ the garage.
- B. ☐ Rachel's room.
- C. ☐ the kitchen.
- D. ☐ the garden.

Q5) The dog kennel is
- A. ☐ near the gate.
- B. ☐ next to the fountain.
- C. ☐ under an apple tree.
- D. ☐ in the garage.

Tratto da www.invalsi.it

3 TASK 8

FAVOURITE ANIMALS

Listen to a group of children talking about their favourite animals.
While listening, put a cross (X) on "YES" if they talk about that animal (A-I), put a cross (X) on "NO" if they don't talk about that animal.
The first one (A) is an example.
You will hear the recording twice.
You will have 20 seconds at the end of the second recording to complete your answers.
You now have 20 seconds to look at the task.

Guarda con attenzione le immagini e pensa ai nomi degli animali che vedi.
Mentre ascolti, fai una crocetta su YES sotto agli animali di cui sentirai parlare; sotto agli animali di cui non si parla dovrai mettere una crocetta su NO.
Concentrati e ce la farai!

A	B	C

YES ☒ NO ☐	YES ☐ NO ☐	YES ☐ NO ☐

D	E	F

YES ☐ NO ☐	YES ☐ NO ☐	YES ☐ NO ☐

G	H	I

YES ☐ NO ☐	YES ☐ NO ☐	YES ☐ NO ☐

Tratto da www.invalsi.it

4 TASK 9

AT THE SCHOOL SPORTS CLUB

Listen to a boy talking with a woman at the school sports club. While listening, choose the correct answer (A, B, C or D) for questions 1-5. Put a cross (X) in the correct box. Only one answer is correct. The first one (0) is an example. You will hear the recording twice. You will have 20 seconds at the end of the second recording to complete your answers. You now have 20 seconds to look at the task.

Sentirai un dialogo tra un ragazzo che vuole iscriversi a un centro sportivo e una signora che raccoglie le iscrizioni. Prima di tutto leggi le domande e osserva attentamente i nomi, le immagini e i numeri. Questo ti aiuterà molto durante l'ascolto. Mentre ascolti, metti una crocetta sotto la risposta giusta. Anche in questo caso ascolterai il brano due volte, perciò calma e concentrazione.

0 What's the woman's name?

A ☐ Sally	B ☒ Sarah	C ☐ Sharon	D ☐ Sue

Q1) What sport does the boy want to play?

A ☐ 	B ☐ 	C ☐ 	D ☐ 

Q2) What's the boy's name?

A ☐ KURT	B ☐ CORT	C ☐ CURT	D ☐ CULT

Q3) How old is the boy?

A ☐ 11	B ☐ 12	C ☐ 20	D ☐ 21

Q4) What is the boy's mum's phone number?

07545315901	07545315902	07545315903	07545315904
A ☐	B ☐	C ☐	D ☐

Q5) What time is the sport lesson?

5:15	5:35	5:45	5:55
A ☐	B ☐	C ☐	D ☐

Tratto da www.invalsi.it

PROVA UFFICIALE 2019 FACSIMILE

TASK 10

FAVOURITE HOBBIES

Listen to some students talking about their favourite hobbies. While listening, choose the hobby (A-H) for each student (1-5). Write your answers in the box. There are two hobbies that you do not need.
The first one (0) is an example.
You will hear the recording twice.
You will have 20 seconds at the end of the second recording to complete your answers.
You now have 20 seconds to look at the task.

Questa volta ci sono 5 studenti che parlano dei loro hobby. Prima di iniziare leggi tutte le frasi della tabella, fai attenzione ai pronomi *he* e *she*. Durante l'ascolto, accanto a ogni immagine scrivi la lettera della frase corrispondente. Concentrati sulla comprensione generale di ciò che viene detto, senza preoccuparti se non capisci subito ogni singola parola. Anche in questo esercizio, ascolterai il testo due volte, perciò se hai qualche indecisione riuscirai a chiarirti ogni dubbio, senza fretta, con calma e... concentrazione!

Speaker		
0		....C....
Q1		....
Q2		....
Q3		....
Q4		....
Q5		....

Hobby	
A	She loves sport.
B	She likes skating.
C	*He likes music.*
D	She likes video games.
E	She likes art.
F	He loves spending time in the kitchen.
G	She loves computer games.
H	She likes watching TV.

Tratto da www.invalsi.it

TASK 1

WANTED

Look at the pictures. Read and complete the sentences (1-6).
Write your answers in the right-hand column.
The first one (0) is an example.

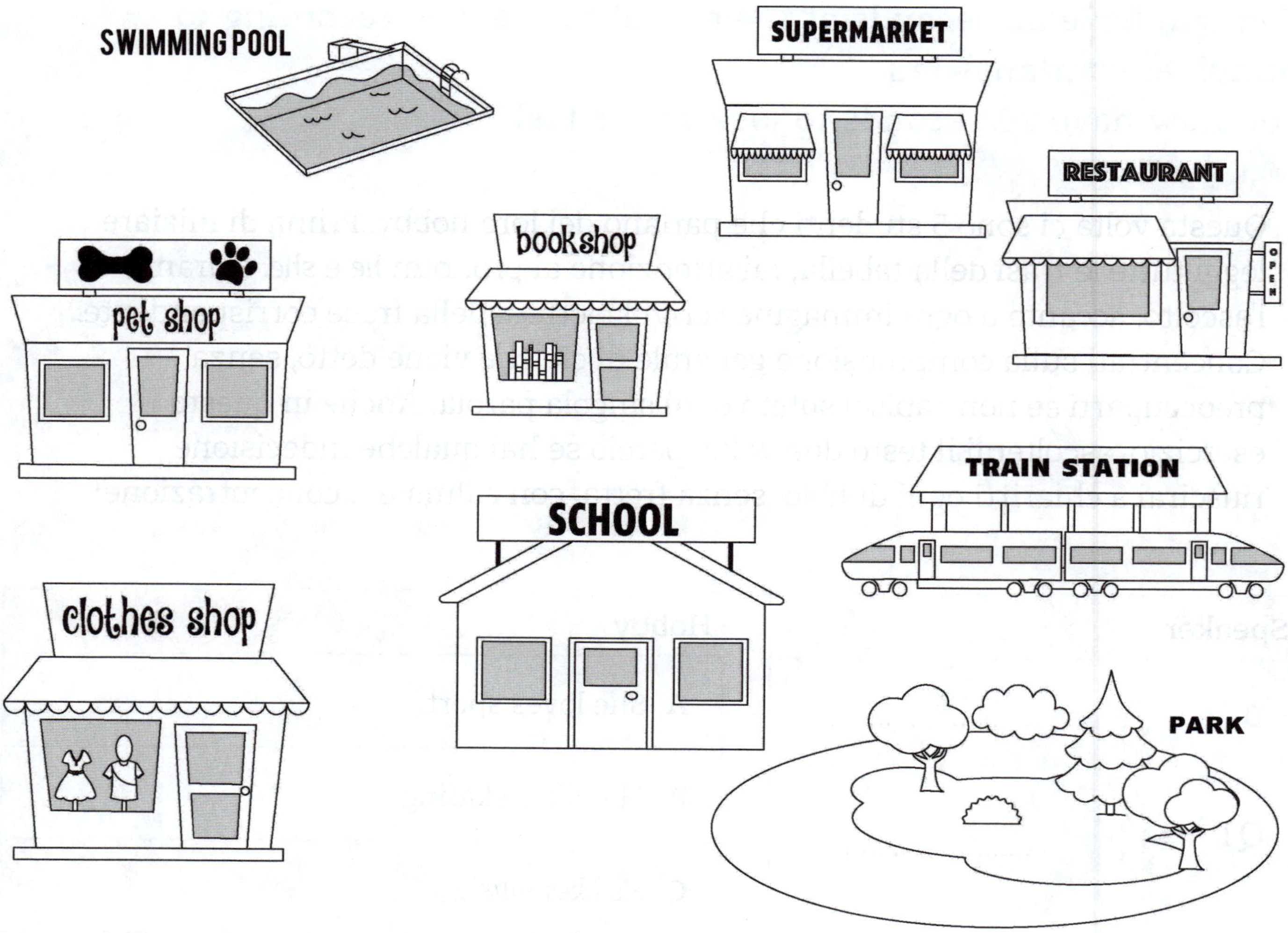

0	*Alex is swimming in the _______.*	*swimming pool*
1	Sarah is buying food for her dog in the _______.	
2	Emily is buying a book in the _______.	
3	Max is having lessons at _______.	
4	Mike and Pam are playing in the _______.	
5	Timmy is looking at a pair of jeans in the _______.	
6	Martina is having lunch at the _______.	

TASK 2

TICKETS

Match the tickets (A-E) with the sentences (1-7). You can use a ticket more than once. Write your answers in the boxes.
The first one (0) is an example.

0	*This ticket was valid for one hour.*	A
1	This ticket was for a child, travelling on a bus.	....
2	This ticket was valid on 28th April.	....
3	This ticket costs more than seventy pounds.	....
4	This ticket was valid for more than six days.	....
5	This ticket was for a group of four people on 27th April.	....
6	This ticket was from Derby to Manchester.	....
7	This ticket was valid on 7th July.	....

TASK 3

AN INVITATION

Read the invitation. Are the sentences (1-7) true, false or not given? Put a cross (X) in the correct box.
The first one (0) is an example.

PARTY INVITATION

WHERE: My house

WHEN: Saturday 23 May

TIME: 6 pm till 10 am

WEAR: Pyjamas

BRING: A sleeping bag

WHY: To celebrate my little brother's birthday

RSVP: Elly 354-08712

	True	False	Not given
0 *The invitation is for a party.*	☒	☐	☐
1 The party is at Elly's house.	☐	☐	☐
2 The party starts on Sunday.	☐	☐	☐
3 The party finishes on Sunday.	☐	☐	☐
4 You can wear jeans at the party.	☐	☐	☐
5 At the party, you can play video games.	☐	☐	☐
6 There is pizza for dinner.	☐	☐	☐
7 The party is for Elly's little brother.	☐	☐	☐

TASK 4

AN AMERICAN GIRL IS TALKING ABOUT HERSELF

Read the text about an American girl and answer the questions (1-7).
Use a maximum of 4 words. Write your answers in the boxes.
The first one (0) is an example.

Hi! I'm Samantha.
I am American. I live in Roseville, California, and I am 12.
I live with my mum, my dad and two brothers.
I love dancing, singing and painting.
I can draw very well, it's my passion. When I grow up, I want to be an artist!
My brother Peter is two years older than me.
He's very good at painting, but his passion is playing the guitar.
When he grows up, he wants to be a musician and form his own rock band.
Patrick is the youngest of the family. He's two years younger than me.
He wants to be a chef.
He says he likes cooking.
He often helps mum and dad in the kitchen.

0 *Name:*	Samantha
1 She is from:	....
2 She wants to be:	....
3 Peter's age:	....
4 He's good at:	....
5 His passion is:	....
6 Patrick's age:	....
7 He wants to be:	....

TASK 5

THE GIANT PANDA

Read about the Giant Panda. Choose the correct answer (A, B, C or D) for questions 1-7. Put a cross (X) in the correct box.
Only one answer is correct.
The first one (0) is an example.

The Giant Panda is the rarest member of the bear family. There are less than 3,000 pandas in the wild and about 270 in zoos and nature reserves. Wild pandas live only in remote, mountainous regions of central China.
They live in thick bamboo forests. Pandas feed on bamboo. They must eat a lot of it every day (about 12 kilograms). Though their diet is 99% bamboo, sometimes they eat flowers, grasses, fruit, honey, eggs, fish or birds. They spend a lot of time – approximately half of the day – looking for food and eating. They are skilled tree-climbers and excellent swimmers. They do not have permanent homes. They sleep at the foot of trees and under rocks. Pandas are solitary animals. At birth, the Giant Panda typically weighs 100 to 200 grams and it is 15 to 17 centimetres long. Adult males can weigh up to 150 kilograms. Females are smaller; they can weigh up to 125 kilograms.

0 ***In zoos and nature reserves, there are...***

A. ☐ about 3,000 pandas.
B. ☐ less than 3,000 pandas.
C. ☒ *about 270 pandas.*
D. ☐ 3,270 pandas.

---

1) **Wild pandas live...**

A. ☐ in Asia.
B. ☐ in Europe.
C. ☐ in Africa.
D. ☐ in America.

2) Pandas...

A. ☐ exclusively eat bamboo.
B. ☐ occasionally eat bamboo.
C. ☐ never eat bamboo.
D. ☐ primarily eat bamboo.

---

3) They...

A. ☐ are very good at climbing trees and swimming.
B. ☐ can't swim.
C. ☐ can't climb trees.
D. ☐ are very good at swimming, but they can't climb trees.

---

4) They live...

A. ☐ in the same home for many years.
B. ☐ in permanent homes.
C. ☐ in temporary homes.
D. ☐ in the same home for one year.

---

5) Pandas prefer...

A. ☐ to live in big groups.
B. ☐ to live in small groups.
C. ☐ to live a solitary life.
D. ☐ to live with animals of different species.

---

6) At birth, pandas...

A. ☐ are less than 15 centimetres long.
B. ☐ are more than 17 centimetres long.
C. ☐ are from 100 to 200 centimetres long.
D. ☐ are between 15 and 17 centimetres long.

---

7) Females pandas...

A. ☐ are usually smaller than males.
B. ☐ are usually bigger than males.
C. ☐ usually weigh up to 150 kilograms.
D. ☐ are always as big as males.

6 TASK 6

WHAT ARE THEY HAVING FOR LUNCH?

Listen to some people talking about their lunch. While listening, write the people's names in the boxes (1-5). There is one picture that you do not need.
The first one (0) is an example.
You will hear the recording twice. You will have 20 seconds at the end of the second recording to complete your answers.
You now have 20 seconds to look at the task.

0) Linda

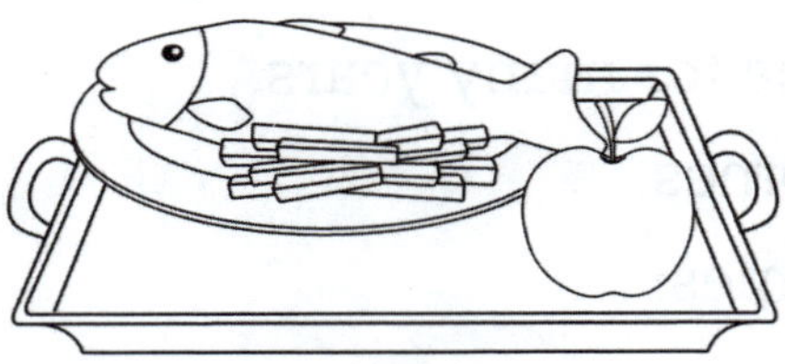

1) ....

2) ....

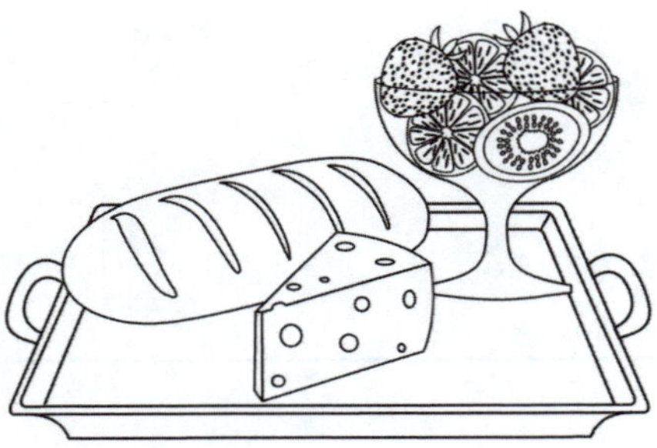

3) ....

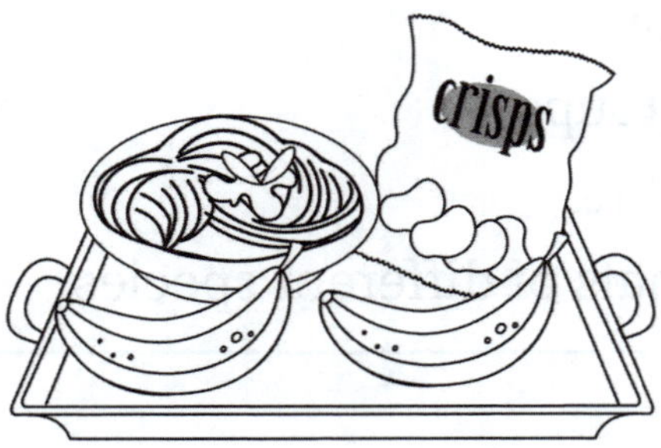

4) ....

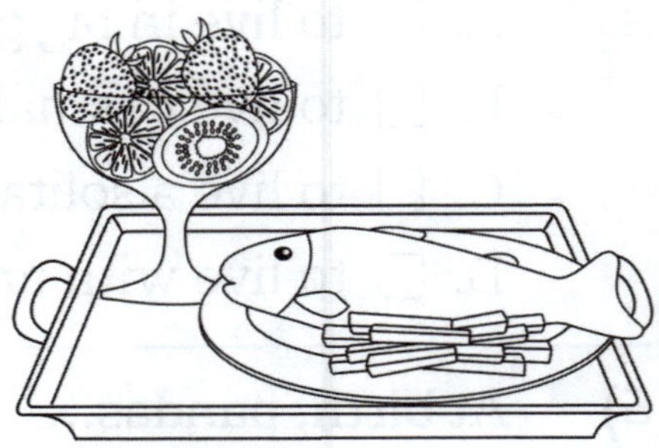

5) ....

TASK 7

BIG BEN

Listen to a woman talking about Big Ben. While listening, choose the correct answer (A, B, C or D) for questions 1-7. Put a cross (X) in the correct box. Only one answer is correct.
The first one (0) is an example.
You will hear the recording twice.
You will have 20 seconds at the end of the second recording to complete your answers. You now have 20 seconds to look at the task.

0 *Big Ben is in...*
- A. ☒ *London.*
- B. ☐ New York.
- C. ☐ Bath.
- D. ☐ Edinburgh.

1) **Big Ben is...**
- A. ☐ a clock.
- B. ☐ a tower.
- C. ☐ a bell.
- D. ☐ a ring.

2) **The tower is near...**
- A. ☐ the Houses.
- B. ☐ the Houses of London.
- C. ☐ the Houses of Big Ben.
- D. ☐ the Houses of Parliament.

3) **The clock helps people...**
- A. ☐ learn English.
- B. ☐ catch buses.
- C. ☐ know the weather.
- D. ☐ know the time.

4) **Big Ben is...**
- A. ☐ 2 metres tall.
- B. ☐ 2.2 metres tall.
- C. ☐ 2 centimetres tall.
- D. ☐ 5 metres tall.

5) **The name of the tower is...**
- A. ☐ Beth.
- B. ☐ Elizabeth.
- C. ☐ Alice.
- D. ☐ Edward.

6) **The clock has four...**
- A. ☐ faces.
- B. ☐ hands.
- C. ☐ feet.
- D. ☐ legs.

7) **At midnight on New Year's Eve, Big Ben rings...**
- A. ☐ 10 times.
- B. ☐ 2019 times.
- C. ☐ 20 times.
- D. ☐ 12 times.

TASK 8

WHAT ARE THEY WEARING?

Listen to the description of some people. While listening, match the pictures (A-F) with their description (1-4). There is one picture that you do not need.
The first one (0) is an example.
You will hear the recording twice. You will have 20 seconds at the end of the second recording to complete your answers.
You now have 20 seconds to look at the task.

		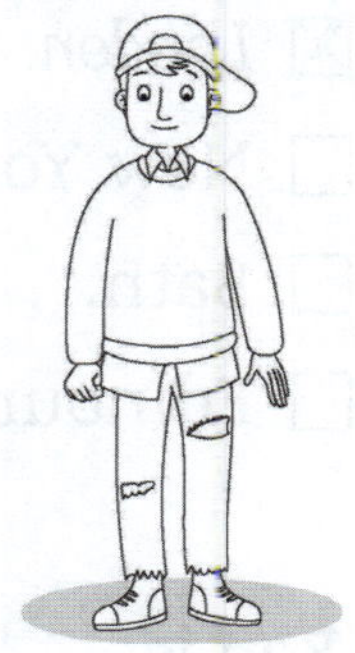
A	B	C

D	E	F

0	1	2	3	4
A				

TASK 9

GUESS THEIR JOBS

Listen to some people talking about their jobs. While listening, choose the correct answer (A, B, C or D) for questions 1-7. Put a cross (X) in the correct box. Only one answer is correct.
The first one (0) is an example.
You will hear the recording twice. You will have 20 seconds at the end of the second recording to complete your answers.
You now have 20 seconds to look at the task.

0

A ☐

B ☐

C [x]

D ☐

1)

A ☐

B ☐

C ☐

D ☐

2)

A ☐

B ☐

C ☐

D ☐

3)

 A ☐
 B ☐
 C ☐
 D ☐

4)

 A ☐
 B ☐

C ☐
 D ☐

5)

 A ☐

B ☐

C ☐
 D ☐

6)

A ☐
 B ☐
 C ☐
 D ☐

7)

 A ☐
 B ☐
 C ☐

D ☐

TASK 10

FAVOURITE SCHOOL SUBJECT

Listen to some students talking about their favourite school subjects. While listening, choose the subject (A-H) for each student (1-5). Write your answers in the box. There are two subjects that you do not need. The first one (0) is an example.
You will hear the recording twice.
You will have 20 seconds at the end of the second recording to complete your answers.
You now have 20 seconds to look at the task.

Speaker		
0		B
1		....
2		....
3		....
4		....
5		....

Favourite school subjects.
A Her favourite subject is Maths.
B *Her favourite subject is Art.*
C His favourite subject is Science.
D His favourite subject is French.
E Her favourite subject is P.E.
F His favourite subject is Geography.
G Her favourite subject is Music.
H His favourite subject is History.

TASK 1

MY HOUSE

Look at this house. Read and complete the sentences (1-6). Write your answers in the right-hand column.
The first one (0) is an example.

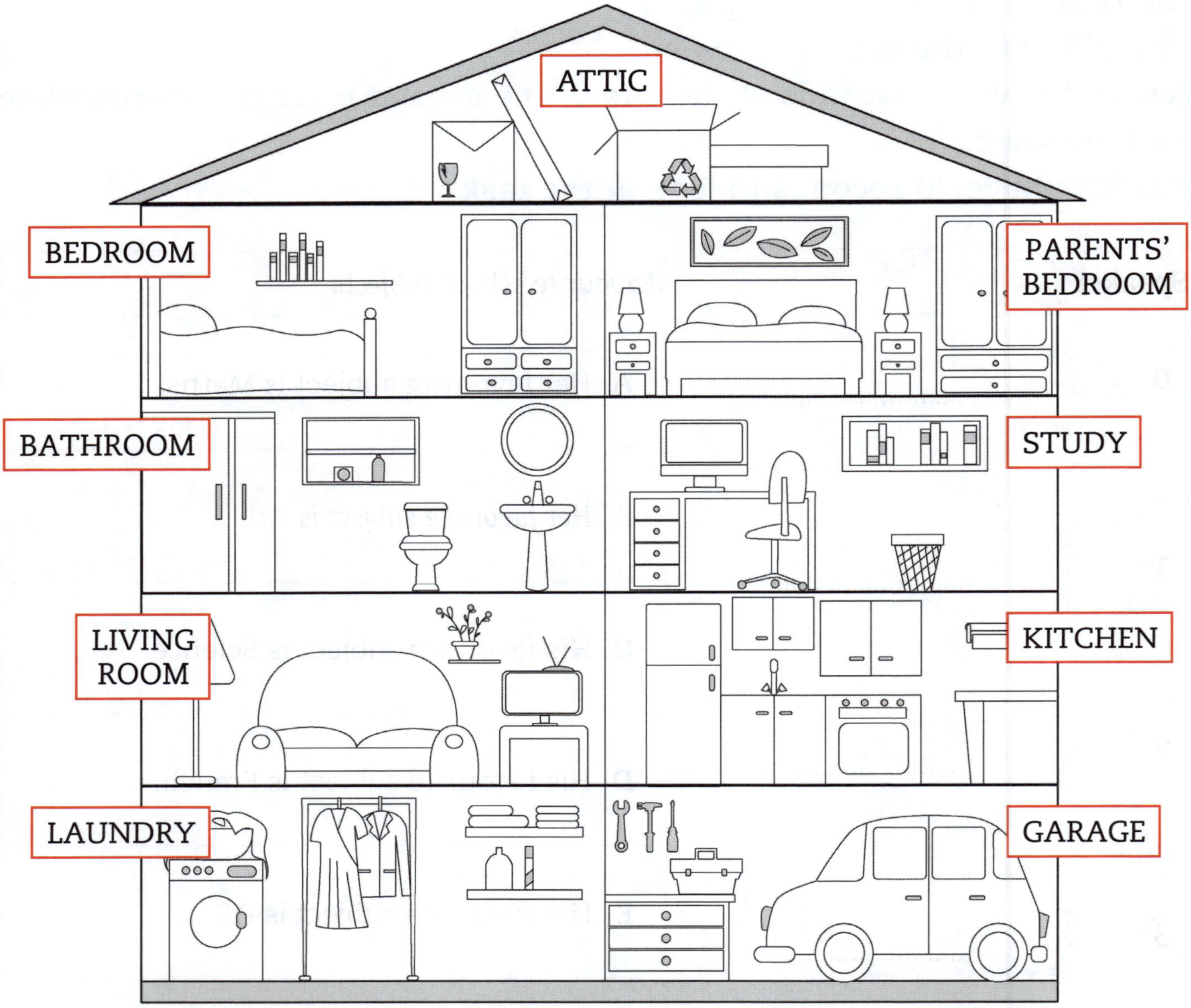

0	*There is a shower in the ___________.*	*bathroom*
1	My dad's car is in the ___________.	
2	I do my homework in the ___________.	
3	I can cook in the ___________.	
4	I can watch TV in the ___________.	
5	I go to bed in my ___________.	
6	Mum washes our clothes in the ___________.	

TASK 2

LET'S GO TO THE CINEMA

Read the film poster. Are the sentences (1-7) true, false or not given? Put a cross (X) in the correct box.
The first one (0) is an example.

		True	False	Not given
0	*It is a film poster.*	X		
1	The film is at the Odeon Cinema.			
2	You can go to the cinema on Monday.			
3	On Friday the film starts at 8.00 p.m.			
4	You can watch the film on Tuesday morning.			
5	Families can get a discount.			
6	It is an American film.			
7	You can buy something to eat.			

TASK 3

CAN YOU READ THESE ROAD SIGNS?

Match the pictures (A-I) with the sentences (1-6). There are two pictures that you do not need. Write your answers in the boxes. The first one (0) is an example.

A	B	C

D	E	F
	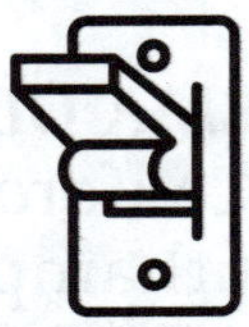	
G	H	I

0	*First aid station.*
1	No bicycles, rollerblades or skateboards in the playground.
2	Protect your environment. Place litter in the bin.
3	No ball games allowed in this area.
4	Emergency exit.
5	A person with a disability can use this toilet.
6	There is a hospital in this area.

0	1	2	3	4	5	6
A						

TASK 4

THE BRITISH MUSEUM

Read the text about the British Museum. Choose the correct answer (A, B, C or D) for questions 1-7. Put a cross (X) in the correct box. The first one (0) is an example.

The British Museum in London contains objects about human history, art and culture. It is free. The museum covers ninety-two thousand square metres. There are one hundred and ninety-four rooms open to the public. It has more than eight million objects, but visitors can only see one per cent of the objects as there are too many to see all together. Nearly seven million people come every year to see the objects. In the museum you can see many artefacts from Egypt. Only the Egyptian Museum in Cairo, Egypt, has more. There is also the very quiet, original Reading Room here too.

0 ***The British Museum is in...***

A. ☐ Paris.

B. ☒ *London.*

C. ☐ Rome.

D. ☐ Scotland.

---

1) It contains objects about...

A. ☐ human culture.

B. ☐ animal culture.

C. ☐ vegetable culture.

D. ☐ tree culture.

---

2) To visit the museum, each ticket costs...

A. ☐ 1 pound.

B. ☐ 1 euro.

C. ☐ nothing.

D. ☐ 10 pounds.

3) **The floor of the museum is...**

A. ☐ 192,000 square metres.

B. ☐ 92,000 square metres.

C. ☐ 9 and 2 square metres.

D. ☐ 29 square metres.

4) **The number of rooms open to the public is...**

A. ☐ less than 100.

B. ☐ 100.

C. ☐ more than 200.

D. ☐ less than 200.

5) **A visitor can see...**

A. ☐ none of the museum's objects.

B. ☐ all of the museum's objects.

C. ☐ not many of the museum's objects.

D. ☐ one hundred of the museum's objects.

6) **The British Museum has...**

A. ☐ more Egyptian objects than the museum in Cairo.

B. ☐ fewer Egyptian objects than the museum in Cairo.

C. ☐ no Egyptian objects.

D. ☐ the same number of Egyptian objects as the museum in Cairo.

7) **The Reading Room in the British Museum is...**

A. ☐ loud.

B. ☐ empty.

C. ☐ new.

D. ☐ old.

TASK 5

SALLY'S WARDROBE

Read the text about a girl's wardrobe. Are the sentences (1-7) true, false or not given? Put a cross (X) in the correct box.
The first one (0) is an example.

Dear Maria,

Thanks for your email. Here is the description of my wardrobe. I've got a big wardrobe full of clothes. I love clothes! I've got twelve pairs of trousers including jeans and twenty-two different T-shirts. For parties I've got three skirts and four dresses. I've got six pretty shirts, and one big old shirt that I keep for when I do crafts at home, a type of apron to protect my clothes. I've got three jackets for summer and two for winter. I've got eight jumpers for summer and winter.

Tell me about your clothes!
Love,
Susie

		TRUE	FALSE	NOT GIVEN
0	*The email is from Susie.*	X		
1	Susie doesn't like clothes.			
2	Susie's got 4 pairs of jeans.			
3	All her T-shirts are pink.			
4	She's got special clothes for parties.			
5	She wears a shirt when she does arts and crafts.			
6	She's got 5 jackets.			
7	She's got 4 jumpers for summer.			

11

TASK 6

LISA AND HER FRIENDS

Listen to Lisa describing her friends. While listening, write the people's names in the boxes (1-4).
The first one (0) is an example.
You will hear the recording twice. You will have 20 seconds at the end of the second recording to complete your answers.
You now have 20 seconds to look at the task.

12 TASK 7

WEATHER AROUND THE WORLD

Listen to a TV programme about the weather. While listening fill in the form. Use a maximum of 4 words. Write your answers in the boxes.
The first one (0) is an example.
You will hear the recording twice.
You will have 20 seconds at the end of the second recording to complete your answers.
You now have 20 seconds to look at the task.

Weather around the world

Sydney	0	beautiful and sunny
	1	
Berlin	2	
	3	
Buenos Aires	4	
	5	
London	6	
	7	

13 TASK 8

SPORTS LESSONS

Listen to a conversation between a boy and a receptionist at the information desk at a sports centre. While listening, choose the correct answer (A, B, C or D) for questions 1-7. Put a cross (X) in the correct box. Only one answer is correct.
The first one (0) is an example.
You will hear the recording twice. You will have 20 seconds at the end of the second recording to complete your answers.
You now have 20 seconds to look at the task.

0 *The boy wants to learn...*

A. ☐ how to play football.
B. ☒ *how to swim.*
C. ☐ how to play tennis.
D. ☐ how to play basketball.

---

1) **The boy is...**

A. ☐ 9 years old.
B. ☐ 10 years old.
C. ☐ 11 years old.
D. ☐ 12 years old.

---

2) **The boy...**

A. ☐ can't swim at all.
B. ☐ can swim well.
C. ☐ can swim and dive
D. ☐ can't swim well.

3) **The boy wants to join...**

A. ☐ the beginner's class.
B. ☐ the elementary class.
C. ☐ the intermediate class.
D. ☐ the advanced class.

4) **There are classes...**

A. ☐ every day.
B. ☐ twice a day.
C. ☐ twice a week.
D. ☐ on Mondays and on Saturdays.

5) **How long are the lessons?**

A. ☐ 40 minutes.
B. ☐ 45 minutes.
C. ☐ 55 minutes.
D. ☐ 14 minutes.

6) **For the lessons the boy must wear...**

A. ☐ a swimsuit.
B. ☐ a t-shirt.
C. ☐ a watch.
D. ☐ a cap.

7) **At the end, the receptionist gives him...**

A. ☐ a computer.
B. ☐ a leaflet.
C. ☐ a book.
D. ☐ a video.

14 TASK 9

WHAT ARE YOU AFRAID OF?

Listen to a group of children talking about what they are afraid of. While listening, put a cross on "YES" if they talk about a fear (A-I), put a cross on "NO" if they don't talk about the fears.
The first one (A) is an example.
You will hear the recording twice.
You will have 20 seconds at the end of the second recording to complete your answers.
You now have 20 seconds to look at the task.

A	B	C

YES ☒ NO ☐	YES ☐ NO ☐	YES ☐ NO ☐

D	E	F

YES ☐ NO ☐	YES ☐ NO ☐	YES ☐ NO ☐

G	H	I

YES ☐ NO ☐	YES ☐ NO ☐	YES ☐ NO ☐

15 TASK 10

WHERE DO THEY COME FROM?

Listen to some students talking about the town they come from. While listening, choose the countries (A-H) for each student (1-5). Write your answers in the box. There are two countries that you do not need.
The first one (0) is an example.
You will hear the recording twice. You will have 20 seconds at the end of the second recording to complete your answers. You now have 20 seconds to look at the task.

Speaker		
0		....C....
1		....
2		....
3		....
4		....
5		....

Countries	
A	He comes from France.
B	He comes from Italy.
C	*He is from Spain.*
D	She comes from Germany.
E	He comes from Mexico.
F	She comes from Japan.
G	She is from Australia.
H	She comes from South Africa.

TASK 1

JOBS

Look at these people and their jobs. Read and complete the sentences (1-6). Write your answers in the right-hand column. There is one picture you don't need.
The first one (0) is an example.

BAKER	PILOT	FIREFIGHTER

DOCTOR	POSTMAN	GARDENER

MECHANIC	NURSE	

0	*I love to work with plants and flowers. I am a ______.*	*gardener*
1	I work in the post office. I am a _____.	
2	I fly an aeroplane in the sky. I am a ___________.	
3	I bake bread, biscuits and cakes. I am a ___________.	
4	I repair cars and motorbikes. I'm a ______________.	
5	I put out fires. I am a _________.	
6	I help the doctor and take care of sick people. I am a _____.	

TASK 2

MY FATHER'S ROUTINE

Read the text about a boy's father. Choose the correct answer (A, B, C or D) for questions 1-6. Put a cross (X) in the correct box. Only one answer is correct.
The first one (0) is an example.

My father usually gets up at four o'clock in the morning. He has a cup of tea and then he starts work. He walks to work. He milks the cows. There are eighty-two cows on the farm. When he finishes he comes back home and eats breakfast. Then he goes around the farm on his motorbike to check the animals and the fields. In the afternoon he milks the cows again and then he comes home to have a shower and have dinner. He goes to bed at nine o'clock.

0 ***My father gets up at...***

A. ☐ 02:00
B. ☐ 03:00
C. ☒ 04:00
D. ☐ 04:30

---

1) For breakfast my father drinks...

A. ☐ milk.
B. ☐ juice.
C. ☐ coffee.
D. ☐ tea.

---

2) He goes to work...

A. ☐ on foot.
B. ☐ by car.
C. ☐ by bus.
D. ☐ on a horse.

3) My father has...

A. ☐ 72 cows.

B. ☐ 82 cows.

C. ☐ 82 dogs.

D. ☐ 82 sheep.

---

4) To check the animals, my father uses...

A. ☐ a bike.

B. ☐ a horse.

C. ☐ a motorbike.

D. ☐ a dog.

---

5) My father milks the cows...

A. ☐ in the morning.

B. ☐ in the afternoon.

C. ☐ in the morning and the afternoon.

D. ☐ never.

---

6) He has dinner...

A. ☐ after his shower.

B. ☐ before his shower.

C. ☐ during his shower.

D. ☐ before breakfast.

TASK 3

AT THE RESTAURANT

Read the menu of an Italian restaurant. Are the sentences (1-7) true, false or not given? Put a cross (X) in the correct box.
The first one (0) is an example.

Casa Italia
Italian restaurant
San Diego - California - USA

• *Starters*

Green salad	$ 3.50
Mozzarella sticks	$ 3.75
Vegetable soup	$ 4.00
Grilled mushrooms	$ 5.00

• *Main Courses*

Lasagna	$ 9.00
Grilled chicken	$ 9.00
Lamb chops	$ 9.50
Pasta with tomato sauce	$ 7.00
Steak	$ 8.50

• *Side Dishes*

Chips	$ 2.00
Baked potatoes	$ 2.50
Peas	$ 2.50
Grilled vegetables	$ 3.50

• *Desserts*

Apple pie	$ 3.00
Ice cream	$ 3.25
Chocolate cake	$ 4.25
Lemon pie	$ 3.20

• *Drinks*

Mineral water	$ 2.00
Beer	$ 4.50
Wine (red or white)	$ 7.00
Soft drinks	$ 2.00
Coffee	$ 3.50

	True	False	Not given
0 *This is the menu of an English Restaurant.*	☐	☒	☐
1 The Restaurant is in Kensington Street.	☐	☐	☐
2 The vegetable soup is the cheapest starter.	☐	☐	☐
3 Lasagna is more expensive than pasta.	☐	☐	☐
4 Baked potatoes cost as much as peas.	☐	☐	☐
5 You can get two desserts with $6.	☐	☐	☐
6 Wine is the most expensive drink served in this restaurant.	☐	☐	☐
7 Children normally get a discount in this restaurant.	☐	☐	☐

TASK 4

SWIMMING POOL RULES

Read the swimming pool rules (A-G) and match them with the sentences (1-5). There is one letter you do not need. Write your answers in the boxes.
The first one (0) is an example.

A

B

C

D

E

F

G

0	*Dogs and cats cannot enter the pool.*	*A*
1	Diving is not permitted. Always use the stairs to enter the pool.	
2	You cannot eat or drink by the pool.	
3	Always have a shower before you enter the pool.	
4	Leave the pool before 10 pm.	
5	Do not throw rubbish in the pool.	

TASK 5

SHERLOCK HOLMES

Read the text about Sherlock Holmes. Answer the questions (1-6). Use a maximum of 4 words. Write your answers in the boxes. The first one (0) is an example.

Sherlock Holmes was a famous detective. He smoked a pipe and played the violin when he wanted to relax. His best friend was Doctor Watson who also accompanied him when he travelled to solve crimes. They lived at 221B Baker Street in London. Sherlock Holmes was a good observer and so he was able to help the police, especially Scotland Yard, the headquarters of the police in London. Sherlock Holmes travelled all over Great Britain to solve crimes and help the police. Sherlock Holmes did not exist in reality; he was an invention of the writer Arthur Conan Doyle.

0 *What was Sherlock Holmes's job?*	*Detective*
1 What musical instrument did he play?	....
2 Who travelled with him when he worked?	....
3 What was their address?	....
4 What is the name of the main Police Station in London?	....
5 Did Sherlock Holmes always work in Scotland?	....
6 Who invented Sherlock Holmes?	....

TASK 6

IN A CLOTHES SHOP

Listen to a conversation between a boy and a shop assistant.
While listening, choose the correct answer (A, B, C or D) for questions 1-4. Put a cross (X) in the correct box. Only one answer is correct.
The first one (0) is an example.
You will hear the recording twice. You will have 20 seconds at the end of the second recording to complete your answers. You now have 20 seconds to look at the task.

0 What does the boy want to buy?

A ☐	B ☐	C ☒	D ☐

1) Which size is the boy?

small	medium	large	extra large
A ☐	B ☐	C ☐	D ☐

2) How much does he pay for the first item of clothing?

£ 5	£ 15	£ 25	£ 50
A ☐	B ☐	C ☐	D ☐

3) What else does he want to buy?

A ☐	B ☐	C ☐	D ☐

4) How much does he pay for the second item of clothing?

£ 35	£ 12	£ 20	£ 22
A ☐	B ☐	C ☐	D ☐

17 TASK 7

CHESSINGTON WORLD OF ADVENTURES

Listen to a dialogue between a girl and her mum.
While listening, choose the correct answer (A, B, C or D) for questions 1-7. Put a cross (X) in the correct box. Only one answer is correct.
The first one (0) is an example.
You will hear the recording twice. You will have 20 seconds at the end of the second recording to complete your answers. You now have 20 seconds to look at the task.

0 ***Today the weather is...***

A. ☐ rainy.
B. ☐ stormy.
C. ☐ cloudy.
D. ☒ *sunny.*

---

1) At Chessington World of Adventures you can see...

A. ☐ sheep.
B. ☐ eagles.
C. ☐ goldfish.
D. ☐ dragons.

---

2) At Chessington World of Adventures...

A. ☐ the lions are in the Antarctic area.
B. ☐ the lions and penguins are together.
C. ☐ the lions are in the safari area.
D. ☐ the penguins are in the safari area.

3) At Chessington World of Adventures...

A. ☐ the butterflies and parrots can't fly.
B. ☐ the butterflies and parrots fly on the ground.
C. ☐ you can't see butterflies and parrots.
D. ☐ you can see butterflies and parrots in the air.

---

4) There are...

A. ☐ 13 rides.
B. ☐ 14 rides.
C. ☐ over 40 rides.
D. ☐ over 50 rides.

---

5) The name of one ride is...

A. ☐ Scorpion Express.
B. ☐ Tarantula Express.
C. ☐ London Express.
D. ☐ School Express.

---

6) The safari has animals from...

A. ☐ England.
B. ☐ Australia.
C. ☐ Africa.
D. ☐ America.

---

7) The animals on the safari are...

A. ☐ water animals.
B. ☐ not dangerous.
C. ☐ dangerous.
D. ☐ tall animals.

18 TASK 8

HOBBIES

Listen to some people talking about their hobbies. While listening, write the people's names in the boxes (1-5). There is one picture that you do not need.
The first one (0) is an example.
You will hear the recording twice. You will have 20 seconds at the end of the second recording to complete your answers. You now have 20 seconds to look at the task.

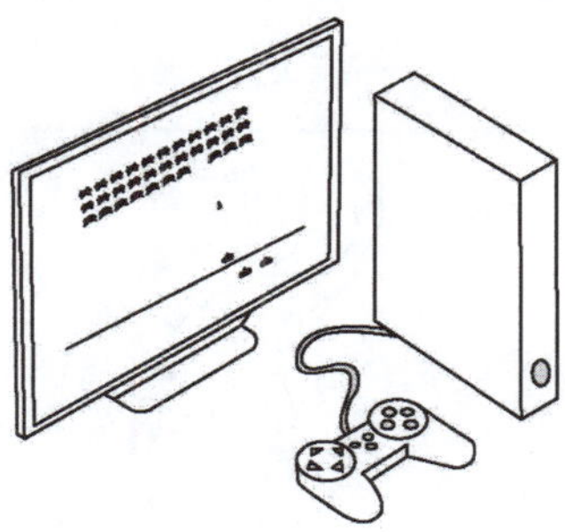

0 Tom

1

2

3

4

5

19 TASK 9

WHAT'S YOUR FAVOURITE SPORT?

Listen to a group of children talking about their favourite sport. While listening, put a cross on "YES" if they talk about a sport (A-I), put a cross on "NO" if they don't talk about the sports.
The first one (A) is an example.
You will hear the recording twice. You will have 20 seconds at the end of the second recording to complete your answers. You now have 20 seconds to look at the task.

A	B	C

YES ☒ NO ☐	YES ☐ NO ☐	YES ☐ NO ☐

D	E	F
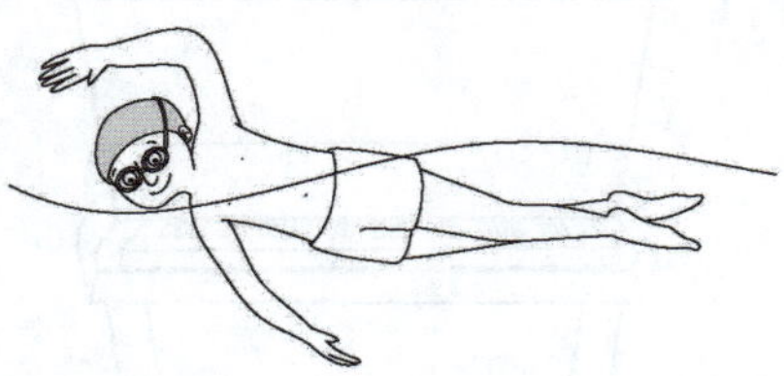		
YES ☐ NO ☐	YES ☐ NO ☐	YES ☐ NO ☐

G	H	I

YES ☐ NO ☐	YES ☐ NO ☐	YES ☐ NO ☐

20 TASK 10

WHAT KIND OF HOUSE DO YOU LIVE IN?

Listen to some students talking about the house they live in. While listening, choose the house (A-H) for each student (1-5). Write your answers in the box. There are two houses that you do not need.
The first one (0) is an example.
You will hear the recording twice. You will have 20 seconds at the end of the second recording to complete your answers. You now have 20 seconds to look at the task.

Speaker		
0		D
1		....
2		....
3		....
4		....
5		....

Houses
A He lives in an igloo.
B He lives in a tent.
C She lives in a bungalow.
D *He lives in a cottage.*
E She lives in a semi-detached house.
F He lives in a skyscraper.
G She lives in a castle.
H She lives in a block of flats.

TASK 1

BOOKS

Look at these books. Read and complete the sentences (1-6).
Write your answers in the right-hand column.
The first one (0) is an example.

0	*Alina is very romantic.* *She likes reading _____.*	*love stories*
1	Flora is a fan of Mickey Mouse. She likes reading _____.	
2	Alex likes stories about zombies and monsters. He likes reading _____.	
3	Max likes spy stories. He likes reading _____.	
4	Pam likes stories of extra-terrestrial invasions. She like reading _____.	
5	Paul plays many sports. He likes reading _____.	
6	Nancy likes animals. She likes reading _____.	

TASK 2

READ ABOUT DAVID, AN ENGLISH BOY

Read the text about an English boy. Choose the correct answers (A, B, C or D) for questions 1-6. Put a cross (X) in the correct box. Only one answer is correct.
The first one (0) is an example.

David is a thirteen-year-old boy.
He lives in Blackpool, with his parents and his younger sister, in a nice house by the sea. In David's house, on the first floor, there is a kitchen, a living room, a dining room and a bathroom. On the second floor, there are two bedrooms and two bathrooms. David is in the dining room.
He is having lunch with his family. He is eating roast chicken and drinking a coke. His sister is eating spaghetti. On the table, there are bananas, oranges, and grapes. David loves bananas, but he doesn't like oranges.
David loves animals very much. He has a dog at home. Its name is Thor. It is his favourite animal. He often plays with it in the garden.

0 *How old is David?*

11	12	13	14
A ☐	B ☐	C ☒	D ☐

1) He lives with...

A ☐

B ☐

C ☐

D ☐

2) He lives in...

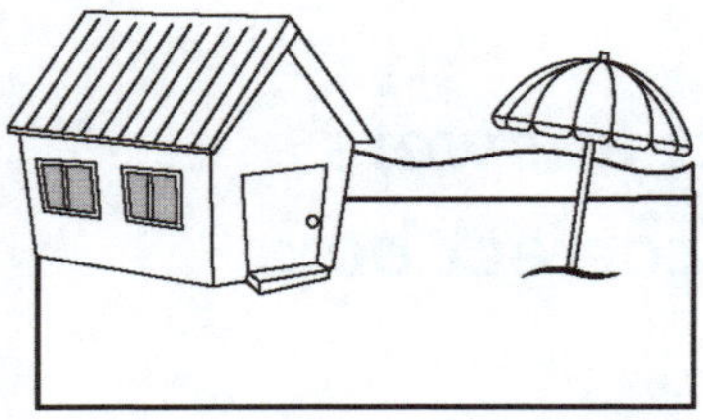
A ☐

B ☐

C ☐

D ☐

3) He is in...

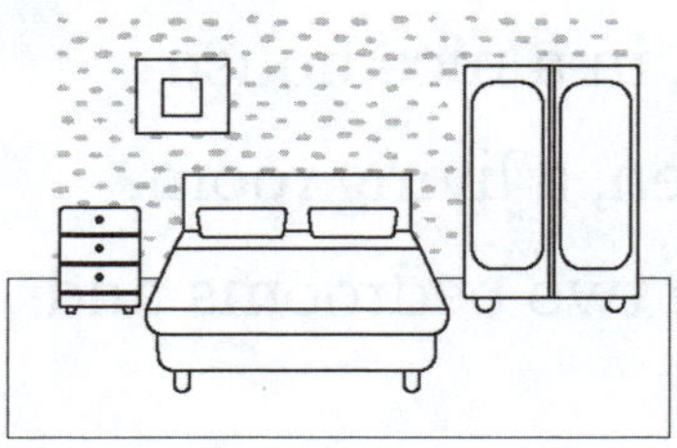
A ☐

B ☐

C ☐

D ☐

4) He is eating with...

A ☐

B ☐

C ☐

D ☐

5) His sister is eating...

A ☐

B ☐

C ☐

D ☐

6) David's favourite animal is...

A ☐

B ☐

C ☐

D ☐

TASK 3

CHARLIE CHAPLIN

Read the text about Charlie Chaplin. Are the sentences (1-7) true, false or not given? Put a cross (X) in the correct box.
The first one (0) is an example.

Charlie Chaplin was an English comic actor, film maker and music composer.
His parents were actors and singers.
He had an older brother, Sydney John, and a younger one, George.
Charlie Chaplin had a difficult childhood, but his passion for singing and acting helped him overcome his difficulties.

	True	False	Not given
0 *Charlie Chaplin was born in the USA.*	☐	☒	☐
1 He wrote music.	☐	☐	☐
2 His father was an actor and a singer.	☐	☐	☐
3 His mother was very famous.	☐	☐	☐
4 He was the youngest of three.	☐	☐	☐
5 His brother Sydney John was older than him.	☐	☐	☐
6 His brother George was an actor, too.	☐	☐	☐
7 When he was a child, he loved singing and acting.	☐	☐	☐

TASK 4

SCHOOL SUBJECTS

Match the pictures (A-I) with the sentences (1-6). There are two pictures that you do not need. Write your answers in the boxes. The first one (0) is an example.

	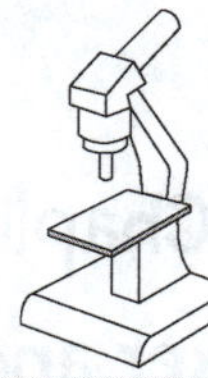	2+24= 26
A	B	C

D	E	F
	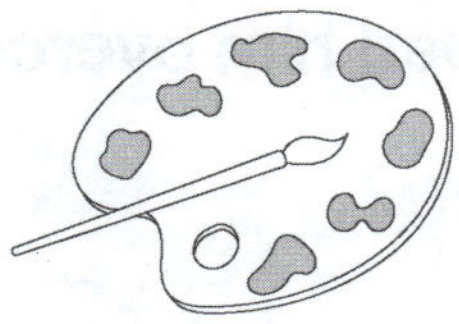	
G	H	I

0	*In this school subject, we learn about different cities and regions in our country.*
1	In this school subject, we learn about the past.
2	In this school subject, we learn how to use technology.
3	In this school subject, we play sports.
4	In this school subject, we learn a foreign language.
5	In this school subject, we learn addition, multiplication and fractions.
6	In this school subject, we draw, colour and paint.

0	1	2	3	4	5	6
A						

TASK 5

THE LONDON EYE

Read the text about the London Eye. Answer the questions (1-6). Use a maximum of 4 words. Write your answers in the boxes. The first one (0) is an example.

The London Eye is a large Ferris wheel, a type of bicycle wheel, but much bigger. It is 135 metres high and its diameter is 120 metres. It has 32 capsules, but no number thirteen because people say thirteen is unlucky. Each capsule can have 25 people in it. The London Eye goes around at 26 centimetres a second. It takes 30 minutes to complete the circle. It does not stop, so you get into the capsule when the wheel is moving. You can walk around or sit down in the capsule. On the wheel you can see all of London.

0 *Where is the London Eye?*	*In London*
1 How tall is the wheel?	....
2 Which number is not on the capsules?	....
3 How many people can go into each capsule?	....
4 How long does one complete circle take?	....
5 Does the London Eye stop?	....
6 Can you walk around in the capsule?	....

21 TASK 6

A PRESENT FOR A FRIEND

Listen to a girl talking to her father about a present for a friend. While listening, choose the correct answer (A, B, C or D) for questions 1-4. Put a cross (X) in the correct box. Only one answer is correct.
The first one (0) is an example.
You will hear the recording twice. You will have 20 seconds at the end of the second recording to complete your answers.
You now have 20 seconds to look at the task.

0 ***What's the name of Katherine's friend?***

Carmel	Camilla	Christine	Charlotte
A ☐	B ☐	C ☒	D ☐

1) When is her birthday?

Next Saturday	Next Sunday	Next Thursday	Last Saturday
A ☐	B ☐	C ☐	D ☐

2) What's her first present?

A ☐	B ☐	C ☐	D ☐

3) What's her second present?

A ☐	B ☐	C ☐	D ☐

4) Where does she come from?

USA	Spain	Italy	France
A ☐	B ☐	C ☐	D ☐

22

TASK 7

FIND THE THIEVES

Listen to a description of two thieves. While listening, fill in the form (1-7). Use a maximum of 4 words. Write your answers in the boxes. The first one (0) is an example.
You will hear the recording twice. You will have 20 seconds at the end of the second recording to complete your answers.
You now have 20 seconds to look at the task.

THE MAN	
0 Age:	*about 30 years old*
1 Hair:	....
2 ....:	very big
3 Jacket:	....
4 Trousers:	....
THE WOMAN	
5 Age:	....
6 ....:	blue
7 Wearing:	....

23 TASK 8

IN A PET SHOP

Listen to a conversation between a boy and a pet shop assistant.
While listening, choose the correct answer (A, B, C or D) for questions 1-7. Put a cross (X) in the correct box. Only one answer is correct.
The first one (0) is an example.
You will hear the recording twice. You will have 20 seconds at the end of the second recording to complete your answers.
You now have 20 seconds to look at the task.

0 *The boy wants to buy...*

A. ☐ some rabbit food.
B. ☐ some hamster food.
C. ☒ *some dog food.*
D. ☐ some cat food.

1) A big tin of food costs...

A. ☐ £ 5.50.
B. ☐ £ 3.50.
C. ☐ £ 1.50.
D. ☐ £ 2.50.

2) A small tin of food costs...

A. ☐ £ 1.50.
B. ☐ £ 2.00.
C. ☐ £ 2.50.
D. ☐ £ 3.50.

3) He buys...

A. ☐ two big tins.
B. ☐ two small tins.
C. ☐ two big tins and two small tins.
D. ☐ one big tin and one small tin.

4) For the pet food, he spends...

A. ☐ £ 17.
B. ☐ £ 3.70.
C. ☐ £ 7.30.
D. ☐ £ 7.

5) He also buys...

A. ☐ a cat.
B. ☐ a goldfish.
C. ☐ a cage.
D. ☐ a collar.

6) For this second item, he spends...

A. ☐ £ 5.99.
B. ☐ £ 9.55.
C. ☐ £ 15.99.
D. ☐ £ 19.99.

7) At the pet shop, the boy spends...

A. ☐ more than £ 12.
B. ☐ less than £ 12.
C. ☐ £ 5 exactly.
D. ☐ £ 10 exactly.

24 TASK 9

WHAT CAN YOU DO IN THE KITCHEN?

Listen to a group of children talking about what they can do in the kitchen. While listening, put a cross on "YES" if they talk about a food (A-I), put a cross on "NO" if they don't talk about the food.
The first one (A) is an example.
You will hear the recording twice. You will have 20 seconds at the end of the second recording to complete your answers.
You now have 20 seconds to look at the task.

A	B	C

YES ☒ NO ☐	YES ☐ NO ☐	YES ☐ NO ☐

D	E	F

YES ☐ NO ☐	YES ☐ NO ☐	YES ☐ NO ☐

G	H	I
		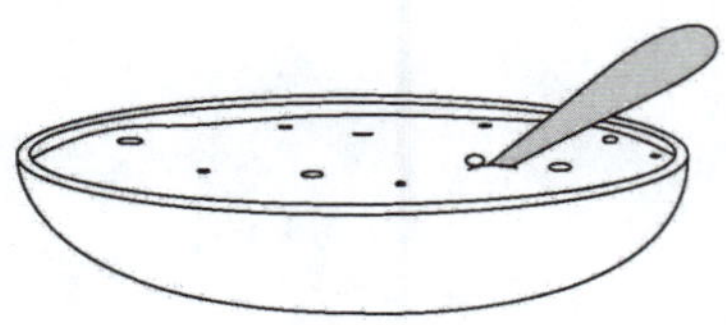
YES ☐ NO ☐	YES ☐ NO ☐	YES ☐ NO ☐

25

TASK 10

TV PROGRAMMES

Listen to some people talking about TV programmes they like. While listening, choose the programme (A-H) for each person (1-5). Write your answers in the box. There are two kind of programmes that you do not need.
The first one (0) is an example.
You will hear the recording twice. You will have 20 seconds at the end of the second recording to complete your answers.
You now have 20 seconds to look at the task.

Speaker		
0		....D....
1		....
2		....
3		....
4		....
5		....

TV *programmes*
A She likes horror films.
B He likes historical films.
C She likes music programmes.
D *She likes the news.*
E He likes sport programmes.
F She likes documentaries.
G He likes the weather forecast.
H He likes romantic movies.

THE PAST SIMPLE TENSE

Il Past simple traduce tre diversi tempi verbali italiani: il **passato prossimo** (*io sono andato*), il **passato remoto** (*io andai*), **l'imperfetto** (*io andavo*).

- Il Past simple si usa per parlare di azioni concluse nel passato.
  She finished her work at seven o'clock.

- Il tempo in cui è avvenuta l'azione può essere un passato lontano ma anche molto vicino.
  One million years ago our planet was very different.
  I saw a red cat one minute ago.

- Il Past simple è associato a determinate espressioni di tempo:
  - often, sometimes, always
    I often had my lunch at school.
    I sometimes walked home at lunchtime.
    I always had milk for breakfast.
  - yesterday, last night, last week, two months ago, when I was six years old
    Yesterday I was at a party.
    We watched a nice movie last night.
    Last week I visited my grandparents.
    Six months ago I went to the seaside.
    She played tennis when she was eight years old.
  - the other day, ages ago, a long time ago
    The other day I met Mrs. Purple.
    Ages ago people lived in caves.
    A long time ago my mother was a nurse.

TO BE – PAST SIMPLE

Forma affermativa	Forma negativa
I was you were he/she/it was we were you were they were	I wasn't you weren't he/she/it wasn't we weren't you weren't they weren't

Forma interrogativa	Risposte brevi	
	Affermative	Negative
was I... ?	Yes, I was.	No, I wasn't.
were you... ?	Yes, you were.	No, you weren't.
was he/she/it... ?	Yes, he/she/it was.	No, he/she/it wasn't.
were we... ?	Yes, we were.	No, we weren't.
were you... ?	Yes, you were.	No, you weren't.
were they... ?	Yes, they were.	No, they weren't.

- Il **Past simple** del verbo essere si costruisce con:
  – **was** per la prima e la terza persona singolare;
  – **were** per tutte le altre persone.
  She was very kind to me.
  You were at the supermarket.
- La forma affermativa è sempre estesa.
  Sono nato/a si traduce con *I was born.*
- La forma negativa del Past simple del verbo essere si costruisce con:
  was / were + not
  I was not tired.
  They were not on the bus.
- La forma negativa può essere estesa *I was not, you were not*, ecc. oppure contratta **I wasn't, you weren't**, ecc.
  I wasn't tired.
  They weren't on the bus.
- La forma interrogativa si costruisce con: **was/were + soggetto**.
  She was happy. = Was she happy?
  They were in Spain. = Were they in Spain?

- Prima del verbo ci può essere una **WH- Question word**: *Why, Who, What, Where, How.*
  Why were you in Africa?
  Who was that boy?
  What was that tool?
  Where were you yesterday?
  How was your summer in Tibet?
- Le **risposte brevi** si costruiscono con:
  – **Yes + soggetto + was / were.**
  – **No + soggetto + wasn't / weren't.**
- Le risposte brevi affermative non hanno la forma contratta.

1) Choose the correct verb.

1 I was – were shorter than now.
2 Mary and Tom wasn't - weren't in town.
3 Was – Were they at the concert?
4 My mother wasn't – weren't a nurse.
5 We was - were good friends.
6 Was – Were Ted at the seaside?

2) Put the words in order and write questions.

1 library the were in they ? ....
2 you lunchtime were ? where at ....
3 with was ? why Max he angry ....
4 friend best ? her were you ....
5 cat was blue it a ? ....
6 sister was ? your she ....

3) Complete. Use *was / were*.

1 Tom .... on holiday with his dad.
2 She .... in her bedroom.
3 That lion .... hungry.
4 We .... at the park.
5 You .... at home.
6 They .... at a party.
7 I .... happy.
8 Ben and Mark .... late.

THE PAST SIMPLE TENSE: VERBI REGOLARI

Forma affermativa	Forma negativa	
I played you played he/she/it played we played you played they played	I didn't play you didn't play he/she/it didn't play we didn't play you didn't play they didn't play	
Forma interrogativa	Risposte brevi	
	Affermative	Negative
Did I play? Did you play? Did he/she/it play? Did we play? Did you play? Did they play?	Yes, I did. Yes, you did. Yes, he/she/it did. Yes, we did. Yes, you did. Yes, they did.	No, I didn't. No, you didn't. No, he/she/it didn't. No, we didn't. No, you didn't. No, they didn't.

- Il Past simple dei verbi regolari si forma aggiungendo **-ed** alla forma base del verbo.
  call ⟶ call**ed**
  watch ⟶ watch**ed**
  cook ⟶ cook**ed**
- Il Past simple ha un'unica forma per tutte le persone:
  *I / you / he / she / it / we / you / they play**ed**.*
- La forma negativa si costruisce con:
  soggetto + didn't + forma base del verbo.
  I didn't call Jack.
  He didn't wash his car.
  We didn't walk to the sports field.
- La forma interrogativa si costruisce con:
  Did + soggetto + forma base del verbo.
  Did you visit your grandparents?
  Did he cook with his dad?
  Did she enjoy the concert?

- Prima di **did** ci può essere una **WH- Question word**: *Why, Who, What, Where, How.*
  Why did she call her teacher?
  Who did you play with?
  What did they watch on TV?
  Where did he wash his dog?
  How did we solve the case?
- Le **risposte brevi** si costruiscono con:
  Yes / No + pronome personale + did / didn't.
- Le risposte brevi affermative non hanno la forma contratta.

Regole di scrittura:
Se un verbo termina in *-e*, si aggiunge *-d*.
agree ⟶ agree**d**
like ⟶ like**d**
escape ⟶ escape**d**

Se un verbo termina con una consonante preceduta da una vocale, di solito la consonante viene raddoppiata prima di aggiungere *-ed*.
stop ⟶ sto**pp**ed
plan ⟶ pla**nn**ed

Se un verbo termina con una consonante seguita da *-y*, si toglie la y e si aggiunge *-ied*.
try ⟶ tr**ied**
carry ⟶ carr**ied**

1) Complete the chart.

Base verb	Past simple	Base verb	Past simple
hop	....	hope	....
hurry	....	spy	....
slip	....	taste	....
joke	....	jog	....

2) Write the sentences in the negative form.

1 I carried that heavy bag home.

....

2 She walked to Matt's house.

....

3 We listened to a beautiful concert.

....

4 They enjoyed my cream cake.

....

5 You painted my old bike.

....

6 He helped his brother.

....

3) Write the sentences in the interrogative form.

1 Our lessons started at 9 o'clock.

....

2 You lived in Australia two years ago.

....

3 I knocked at the door three times.

....

4 He climbed Mount Everest.

....

5 They walked to the swimming pool.

....

6 She washed her mother's car.

....

THE PAST SIMPLE TENSE: VERBI IRREGOLARI

Forma affermativa	Forma negativa	
I went you went he/she/it went we went you went they went	I didn't go you didn't go he/she/it didn't go we didn't go you didn't go they didn't go	
Forma interrogativa	Risposte brevi	
	Affermative	Negative
Did I go? Did you go? Did he/she/it go? Did we go? Did you go? Did they go?	Yes, I did. Yes, you did. Yes, he/she/it did. Yes, we did. Yes, you did. Yes, they did.	No, I didn't. No, you didn't. No, he/she/it didn't. No, we didn't. No, you didn't. No, they didn't.

- Molti verbi in inglese sono irregolari e hanno una forma completamente diversa per il presente e il passato:
  come ⟶ *came* *make* ⟶ *made* *drink* ⟶ *drank*
- Ma per alcuni verbi la forma del presente e del passato sono uguali nella scrittura: *cut, put, cost, hit, hurt, let, read, spread, set*...
  She cuts fruit every day.
  She cut a pineapple yesterday.
- I verbi irregolari seguono le stesse regole dei verbi regolari:
  He met Lisa at school.
  He didn't meet Lisa at school.
  Did he meet Lisa at school?
  Yes, he did. / No, he didn't.
- **WH- Question words:**
  Why did you go out?
  Who did you meet?
  What time did they get up?
  Where did she put her secret diary?
  How did he make that cake?

I VERBI IRREGOLARI PIÙ USATI IN INGLESE

Base form	*Past simple*	*It means*	*Base form*	*Past simple*	*It means*
be	*was/were*	essere	*lose*	*lost*	perdere
begin	*began*	cominciare	*make*	*made*	fare
break	*broke*	rompere	*mean*	*meant*	significare
bring	*brought*	portare	*meet*	*met*	incontrare
buy	*bought*	comprare	*pay*	*paid*	pagare
build	*built*	costruire	*put*	*put*	mettere
choose	*chose*	scegliere	*run*	*ran*	correre
come	*came*	venire	*say*	*said*	dire
cost	*cost*	costare	*see*	*saw*	vedere
cut	*cut*	tagliare	*sell*	*sold*	vendere
do	*did*	fare	*send*	*sent*	inviare
draw	*drew*	disegnare	*sit*	*sat*	sedere
drive	*drove*	guidare	*speak*	*spoke*	parlare
eat	*ate*	mangiare	*spend*	*spent*	spendere
feel	*felt*	sentire	*stand*	*stood*	alzarsi
find	*found*	trovare	*take*	*took*	prendere
get	*got*	ottenere	*teach*	*taught*	insegnare
give	*gave*	dare	*tell*	*told*	dire/raccontare
go	*went*	andare	*think*	*thought*	pensare
have	*had*	avere	*understand*	*understood*	capire
hear	*heard*	sentire (udito)	*wear*	*wore*	indossare
know	*knew*	sapere	*win*	*won*	vincere
leave	*left*	lasciare	*write*	*wrote*	scrivere

1) Complete with the Past simple.

1 We (get up) .... at 9 o'clock.
2 I (meet) .... my aunt.
3 They (have) .... baked beans for lunch.
4 She (send) .... a text to Mariam.
5 He (read) .... a book in English.
6 You (go) .... to the swimming pool.
7 My sister (make) .... a kite.
8 He (take) .... my pen.

2) Write the sentences in the negative form.

1 We wrote a letter to the principal.

....

2 I bought a new jacket.

....

3 She ran a dangerous race.

....

4 He rode his bike to school.

....

5 You gave me a glass of water.

....

6 He took a hundred photos.

....

7 They fell down the stairs.

....

8 I broke a vase.

....

3) Write the sentences using the Present simple.

1 He got very angry with me.

....

2 She took a warm bath after dinner.

....

3 We cut the grass in the garden.

....

4 Tom spoke to his teacher.

....

5 Mary heard the door bell ringing.

....

6 They read a music magazine.

....

THE PAST CONTINUOUS TENSE

Forma affermativa	Forma negativa	
I was playing you were playing he / she / it was playing we were playing you were playing they were playing	I wasn't playing you weren't playing he / she / it wasn't playing we weren't playing you weren't playing they weren't playing	
Forma interrogativa	**Risposte brevi**	
	Affermative	**Negative**
Was I playing? Were you playing? Was he / she / it playing? Were we playing? Were you playing? Were they playing?	Yes, I was. Yes, you were. Yes, he /she /it was. Yes, we were. Yes, you were. Yes, they were.	No, I wasn't. No, you weren't. No, he / she / it wasn't. No, we weren't. No, you weren't. No, they weren't.

Il Past continuous si usa per parlare del passato:

- Per descrivere un'azione che ha avuto una certa durata nel passato:
  *My sister **was listening** to the radio.*
  *All my classmates **were reading**.*
  *The sun **was shining**.*
- Per descrivere un'azione iniziata prima e continuata dopo un'altra azione:
  *We **were doing our homework** when mum got home.*
  *I **was watching** television when the telephone rang.*
- Questo uso del Past continuous è molto comune quando ad esempio si racconta una storia:
  *In the morning Alison and her brother **were walking** to school when…*
  *Yesterday I **was waiting** for my friend Tom when…*
  *Last week I **was playing** volleyball when...*
- Per descrivere due azioni che avvengono contemporaneamente nel passato:
  Max was reading a book while Ella was watching tv.
  We were coming home while my parents were going out.

- Il Past continuous si forma con:
  Past simple of to be + forma -*ing* del verbo.
  He was going to the park.
  He wasn't going to the park.
  Was he going to the park? Yes, he was. No, he wasn't.

1) Write the -*ing* form of the verbs.

1 cry ....
2 go ....
3 cycle ....
4 study ....
5 hop ....
6 sing ....
7 dance ....
8 fry ....

2) Read the chart and write what Ben was doing yesterday at a particular time.

8.10 a.m. - 8.30 a.m.	drive to work
8.30 a.m. - 12 p.m.	work
12.15 p.m. - 12.45 p.m.	have lunch
6.30 p.m. - 7.00 p.m.	cook dinner
7.00 p.m. - 7.10 p.m.	wash the dishes
10.30 p.m. - 6.50 a.m.	sleep

1 At 8.15 a.m. ....
2 At 11.35 a.m. ....
3 At 12.45 p.m. ....
4 At 6.45 p.m. ....
5 At 7.05 p.m. ....
6 At 11.30 p.m. ....

3) What were these people doing when it started raining?
Write the answers.

1 mum / water / the flowers

....

2 dad / drink / coffee

....

3 Jane / wash / her bike

....

4 Dave / jog / in the park

....

5 His grandparents / walk / home

....

6 Their cousins / playing / in the garden

....

7 Ted / climb / a tree

....

8 neighbours / have / a picnic

....

4) ***While*** **or** ***when?***

1 My mum was preparing lunch .... I was doing my homework.
2 I was walking my dog .... I met my English teacher.
3 He was drinking a cup of tea .... a thief got in.
4 .... I saw Tina at the party, she was wearing a beautiful dress.
5 My father was driving .... we were sleeping.
6 The sun was shining .... a rainbow appeared.

5) Complete. Write the correct verbs.

1 I (sleep) .... when my friend (ring) .... the doorbell.
2 While we (sing) .... they (listen)................................ to the radio.
3 She (clean) .... her room when her sister (get) .... in.
4 When we (fall) .... down we (skate) ....
5 He (cook) .... while she (play) .... the piano.
6 I (study) .... while my friends (play) .... football.
7 When the giraffe (look) .... at me I (take) .... a photo.
8 He (cut) .... vegetables when the cat (jump) .... on the table.

THE FUTURE

Si usa il futuro quando si descrive un'azione non ancora avvenuta.
Di solito il verbo al futuro è accompagnato da espressioni come:

- tonight, tomorrow, this afternoon, this evening
- next week, next month, next summer, next year
- on Monday (Tuesday, Wednesday ecc.)

Il futuro italiano si può tradurre in diversi modi:

- con **il presente progressivo**
- con **will**
- con **going to**

IL FUTURO CON IL PRESENTE PROGRESSIVO

Quando un'azione è stata decisa in precedenza, il futuro si traduce con il **presente progressivo.**

I'm leaving by train at three o'clock in the afternoon.
The Red Lions are playing this evening.
I'm meeting Ann at the park.

IL FUTURO CON GOING TO

Quando si esprime **un'intenzione** o si parla del **tempo atmosferico** il futuro si traduce con **going to.**

- La forma **affermativa** del futuro intenzionale si costruisce con:
  soggetto + am/is/are + going to + forma base del verbo principale
  I'm going to call my grandmother.
  They are going to go to the concert.
  It's going to rain.

- La forma **negativa** del futuro intenzionale si costruisce con:
  soggetto + am/is/are + not + going to + forma base del verbo principale
  I'm not going to tell you.
  She's not going to make a cake.
  They're not going to play with me.

- La forma **interrogativa** del futuro intenzionale si costruisce con:
  am/is/are + soggetto + going to + forma base del verbo principale
  Are you going to eat that huge hamburger?
  Are they going to go to the match?
  Is he going to fly a hot-air balloon?

Prima del verbo ci può essere una **WH- Question word:** Why, Who, What, Where, How.
Why are you going to paint your bike?
Who is going to cook pasta?
What are you going to do?
Where is she going to go?
When are you going to do your homework?
How are they going to travel?

- Le **risposte brevi** si usano per rispondere sì / no. Si costruiscono con:
  Yes + soggetto + am / is / are.
  No + soggetto + am not / is not / are not.
- Le risposte brevi affermative non hanno la forma contratta.

1) Complete the short answers.

1 Is she going to write an email? Yes, ...
2 Are you going to ride your bike? No, ...
3 Is he going to have an ice cream? Yes, ...
4 Are they going to have a party? No, ...

2) Rewrite the sentences using the negative form.

1 It's going to snow. ....
2 She's going to cook a delicious meal. ....
3 They're going to be late. ....
4 She's going to paint her room pink. ....
5 He's going to sing in front of the class. ....
6 I'm going to visit the British Museum. ....

3) Put the words in order and write sentences.

1 Are / buy / going / you / to / a new web cam?

....

2 party / go / is / Mary / going / to / not / to / the.

....

3 friends / going / Are / to / visit / July / you / in / your / Mexico?

....

4 this / homework / to / her / Is / Ann / going / afternoon / do.

....

5 dog / going / a / Are / buy / you / to?

....

6 rain / going / it / Is / to?

....

IL FUTURO CON WILL

Quando si prevede un'azione che non dipende da noi, quando si prende una decisione istantanea e quando si fa una promessa o una previsione, il futuro si traduce con il futuro semplice, cioè con **will**.

<table>
<tr><th>Forma affermativa</th><th colspan="2">Forma negativa</th></tr>
<tr><td>I will play.
You will play.
He / She / It will play.
We will play.
You will play.
They will play.</td><td colspan="2">I won't play.
You won't play.
He / She / It won't play.
We won't play.
You won't play.
They won't play.</td></tr>
<tr><th rowspan="2">Forma interrogativa</th><th colspan="2">Risposte brevi</th></tr>
<tr><th>Affermative</th><th>Negative</th></tr>
<tr><td>Will I play?
Will you play?
Will he / she / it play?
Will we play?
Will you play?
Will they play?</td><td>Yes, I will.
Yes, you will.
Yes, he /she /it was.
Yes, we will.
Yes, you will.
Yes, they will.</td><td>No, I won't.
No, you won't.
No, he/she/it wasn't.
No, we won't.
No, you won't.
No, they won't.</td></tr>
</table>

- La **forma contratta** di will è **'ll**.
- La **forma contratta** di will not è **won't**.
- La forma **affermativa** si costruisce con:
  soggetto + will + forma base del verbo principale
  She'll be ten in March.
  He'll pass the exam.
  I'll tell him.
- La forma **negativa** si costruisce con:
  soggetto + will + not + forma base del verbo principale
  In July she will not go to school.
  They will not play the tennis match on Sunday.
  I will not do it.
- La forma **interrogativa** di will si costruisce con:
  will + soggetto + forma base del verbo principale
  Will Lucy go to a summer camp?
  Will your brothers be at home tomorrow?
  Will you play?
- Prima del verbo ci può essere una **WH- Question word:** Why, Who, What, Where, How.
  Who will be the first?
  What time will the match finish?
  Where will we look for your cat?
  When will you call your teacher?
  How many people will be at the concert?
- Le **risposte brevi** si usano per rispondere sì / no. Si costruiscono con:
  Yes + soggetto + will
  No + soggetto + won't
- Le risposte brevi affermative non hanno la forma contratta.
  Will you play at the concert? Yes, I will.
  Will Mary sing at the concert? No, she won't.

1 Rewrite the sentences in the negative form.

1 In July Martina will go to school. ....

2 They will play the match next Saturday. ....

3 Steve will be late. ....

4 Ella will pass the exam. ....

5 I will buy a new I-pod next week. ....

6 The train will be late. ....

2 Rewrite the sentences in the interrogative form, then answer.

1 It will be very expensive.

.... No, ...

2 School will be over next week.

.... Yes, ...

3 Your parents will go to Spain.

.... No, ...

4 You will go with them.

.... No, ...

5 It will take two hours to go to Oslo.

.... Yes, ...

6 She will go to the party.

.... No, ...

7 He will have a lemonade.

.... Yes, ...

8 You will fly to London.

.... Yes, ...